WHERE WE ARE
ALISON FLETT

Other publications by Alison Flett

POETRY

Restricted Vocabulary
Semiosphere
Vessel
Whit Lassyz Ur Inty
Writing Like a Bastard

ALISON FLETT

WHERE

WE

ARF

FLETT

BOOK 01
SERIES 5
CORDITE BOOKS

First printed in 2022
by Cordite Publishing Inc.

PO Box 393
Carlton South 3053
Victoria, Australia
cordite.org.au | corditebooks.org.au

National Library of Australia
Cataloguing-in-Publication:

   Flett, Alison
   Where We Are
   978-0-6489176-7-0 paperback
   I. Title.
   A821.3

Poetry set in Rabenau 10 / 15
Cover design by Zoë Sadokierski
Text design by Kent MacCarter and Zoë Sadokierski
Printed and bound by McPherson's Printing, Maryborough,
Victoria.

10 9 8 7 6 5 4 3 2 1

For my family near and far:

Adrian, Aphra, Maz, Alfie – thank you for being with me on the journey and making it so beautiful.

Mum, Dad, Sheena, Andy, Caroline – thank you for the love and support that set me on the right path.

Freyja, Jamila – thank you for keeping it real.

Love you all, endlessly.

CONTENTS

PREFACE

When I first left my home, the gnawing ache for all I'd left behind – family, friends, my land, my whole life – made me numb and *thrawn*. Weeping and sobbing – *bubblin an greetin,* as you would call it in Scotland – would have been too wet and hand-wringy. What I felt was bone-dry and primal; I wanted to drop to my knees, throw my head back and howl. I pined like an animal, without tears.

Home is different for each of us, made from the sounds words make in our mouths and the thoughts they form in our brains. Made from landscapes, cityscapes, seascapes, the people who gather with us round our fires, the smell the smoke leaves on our skins. Removed from our homes, we must remake not only that place of comfort, but ourselves.

At a time when more than 82 million people worldwide have been violently displaced, it feels wrong to complain about my own privileged emigration to Australia. I didn't need to come, and it was embarrassingly easy. Ticket, visa, then citizenship: all a formality. The greater your need to be here, the harder it is to be accepted.

Nonetheless, coming here was the biggest upheaval of my life, and many of these poems are about the remaking of self and the building of a new home around it.

I share only a minute part of the grief that many recent Australians and asylum-seeking detainees are living with, and even less of the grief that Australia's colonised First Nations must feel. Yet, I understand the immensity of what has been lost and my education is ongoing. To all who have lost their homes: *lang may yir lums reek* (may your fires always burn).

INTRODUCTION

Where We Are is about place (where), people (we) and the present tense of existence (are). The place could be two, Scotland and Australia, but really it's one: wherever we find ourselves. The people could be poet, family and friends, poet and reader, or all of us on this drowning, burning earth. The present tense could be this moment, or a past so intensely remembered, or a future so powerfully imagined that past, present and future are simultaneously here.

Conditional responses to the poems seem not only possible, but necessary. There's much that slips in and out of light, and Flett's poems have a zero-sum gaze: where there's not light, there's darkness. In 'Wherever This Is It's Where We Are', there is 'thedarkthatsurroundsus' and 'the labyrinth of dark streets' and 'the crow's black heart'. There are the hunting shadows of Tenebrae, the service of falling darkness. And the fox's 'wet black pavements' and 'red-black fur' and 'black-red eyes' in 'Semiosphere' (shades of Terrance Hayes's 'black-eyed animal'.) The fox slinks in and out of darkness, in and out of sight and comprehension. Darkness isn't always threatening – it's just that we can't understand inside it.

We read some of these poems as stories, because inventing narrative lines – that may not be there – makes sense. 'Seen Through' is six window views, from living room to B&B to Hilux to tent to pub and home. We read the 'to's into this, they're not written in, making it a traveller's tale, a road trip up the 'Oodnadatta stretch' and on to Uluru and back. 'Still Life in Library with Keys' might seem like a painting, as in Kelman's version of Cézanne's 'les joueurs', but it's alive – it's still life, not a picture of it. It's the story of a poem being written, or unlocked, or emerging, among the millions of words shelved in the library. Brand-new text born out of old but also out of the library's pigeons, passers-by, line dancers, self-talkers, soup-eaters. 'Nothing but noise'? Nah, we hear poetry.

Tomas Tranströmer haunts Irvine Welsh in 'Liminoid', a prose-poem yarn in Edinburgh Scots: 'a tousie bunch' of partygoers glimpsing a fox (that doggone beast again!) out of the corner of an eye. There you go: a second Scottish prose writer, but not a poet in sight, because there's no glimpse of contemporary Scottish poetry here. Twenty-five years ago, Flett's work moved in tight formation with Tom Leonard, Margaret Hamilton and Ian Hamilton Finlay. Now, having flown half way round the world, she's in an orbit with Ken Bolton, John Forbes, Jill Jones, Eileen Myles.

In 'There Is a Bigger Telling That Moves Around the World', words make the world go round: language is 'the ultimate thump thump'. 'Telling' is counting, what a teller does after elections. The vote here was a choice between 'a song of YES' and the 'cold NO' which won. But there's hope for YES next time because 'we have all the words'. Those Australians at their barbecues talk so much that words form a 'tumulus', 'mounded over us'. The great heaps of ancient civilisations are tells. Is that what the builders are shouting about? When we read 'something/that might have been done   was not done', we catch the echo of Scotland's many hill fort duns – Dunbar, Dundee Law, Dùn Èideann. The story goes round: we could have built a castle, but cold NO won, and we didn't. Still, the builders are busy, they're opening the ground. Maybe they're digging to Australia. Or maybe I'm digging up far-fetched meanings. And? You want to make something of it? Go ahead: build.

Here we are with a poet who knits intricate patterns of sound and image, line to line, poem to poem; a poet who pays attention to W=h=e=r=e=W=e=A=r=e and makes it heartbreaking, breathtaking, beautiful.

—Duncan McLean

we're connected, right?
repetitive, birling, one hame
and another, one body and another
sun – moon – city – desert – rain – sea – globe

Versus

For these few moments houstered here on either side
of the railway crossing, waiting for the freight to pass
only minutes though seems like hours, the ding-ding-ding
       the wave
of boom gates, the kicky-de-chick of many wheels, the recoil
       of sleepers
as the rolling stock spanks across, the sunlight flicking between
       containers
skittering across the opposite faces, reminding us of quick-
       fire snapshots
eyes squinting into the camera flash or of swimmers' faces
repeatedly rising from ferrous water, gasping, descending
but then

       the gap of an empty trolley
       its sense of space
       the wider clarity

a girl on our side jumping up and
shouting *train!* the single syllable entering our heads
       turning into
       steam/electric
       freight/passenger
       Ghan/Indian Pacific
the network of tracks criss-crossing the continent
signs and signals – the punctuation, staccato shazam of all that is
conveyed in honks or silently transported

but then

      the girl lifts totie stones
      throws them between the passing boxes
      and a boy opposite does the same
                the stones' parabolas
                    opening pathways
                      of movement
                          between the 90
                            degree boxes
                        opening up
                    with absolute
                freedom and no
              intended destination

while we wait, our minds closed around our own
stones, ready to exchange them in trade, to pass them
as counters in a game or to throw them at the saftish
body, the bruisable flesh, the flaccid organs
or maybe at the hard bits, the brittle scaffold
the inner structure, we don't ken what is
going to happen, only that the train will pass
that our soft-hard bodies will cross over
that another train is already pulling
out of a nearby siding.

Adelaide, I Dream You

Adelaide, I dream you, your cream rollers breaking
apart on your jetties, the raked-clean beaches, sand
tongued white by the Southern Ocean, beachgoers
drinking their flats and lattes, black coffee covered
with steamed white froth. Adelaide, I dream your hot December
your sweaty Christmas parade, Adelaide, your giant plastic
Santa and your blow-up snowmen, is the blinding sun
like the snow, Adelaide? Do you want to make it so?
Your crinoline-frilled history, your spinning-parasol past with corseted
women in Miss Gladys Sym Choon shoes, photochrome postcards
of open streets, the dirt beaten flat over what lies
beneath. What are you trying to hide, Adelaide, in the neatness
of your chart? All laid out in a grid, Adelaide, Hindley St intersecting
your heart, the mango-sweet of Empire Shisha, the neon outlines
of women's bodies, Crazy Horse strippers with synthetic wigs
gawped at by suitboys and men with paunches, the punch and shrill
of gold-filled pokies, pavements stained with puke. Your blood dreams
birl inside me, Adelaide. Do our outsides reflect our insides or is it
the other way round? My face is starting to change, Adelaide, I think I
might be you, your hidden pain, your homesick past, the slap-slap-slap
of those northern suburbs, white salt pans and scrubland paddocks
factories and flat-packed land. Your long straight highways stamped
with billboard warnings, littered with crow-picked roadkill, glistered
with cellophaned grief. I don't ken if I belong. Adelaide, I don't ken
if you belong. What does it mean to belong, Adelaide? D'you remember
how this began? You act like it's all yours, Adelaide, as if
you've always been here, fussing with dusty petticoats, polishing
curlicued balconies. Is forgetting the only solution? The old
me has faded, Adelaide, making me afraid. I think
we can fix this, I do, Adelaide, but we've still got a lot to learn.

Temporary

on th sand
we sittn lickn
our icecreams
sweet flavrs drippn
disapprn
tween th grains
—
under th jetty
a cellophand bouquet
strappd to th upright —
a *descanso* for a child who
got carried off
by a rip
—
in th water
with th kids some guy yell
shark I think
for a joke till I see
the fin the tail flick
get out I say quick
—
on th sand
my youngest ask if
we go in th water
again will it happn again
no I say it wont not
like that

Still Life in Library with Keys   for Ken Bolton

It seems like everywhere
there's nothing
but noise, even here
in the library
where you might expect quiet
there's a man blethering away
to himself, mostly mumping
so you can't hear the words
(what was that he said about trust?)
but occasionally the volume rises
and becomes intrusive

I SAID DON'T TRUST ANYTHING

in the background
there are doors
opening and closing
while outside the window
there's the running engine
of a bus waiting at the lights

inside the bus, the faces are mostly looking down
probably at phones but there's someone looking up
through the bus window, at me, behind
the window of this library in this city
in this country which is not my country
although the notion of my country seems false
as if I could really belong to a bit of land
or it to me

even the notion of me as if I existed
in some concrete way that was more than just atoms

interacting with other atoms seems egotistic
but difficult to shake

on the pavement beside the bus
I can see paving slabs that have rent
and rived where some root or other
has pushed up from underneath
humping the cracked slabs into a trip hazard

one or two of the people on the bus
are also looking
in the direction of this crack
but I don't ken if they're seeing
what I'm seeing

in my country people
are mostly sleeping
because it's a different time
for them, still yesterday

I don't ken
what any of them are seeing

there's a sliding door between the library and
the adjacent community centre
which makes a shh sound as people
come and go, letting music
from the line-dancing class and the thudding
and clapping of people dancing in a line
in and out of the library

(more noise)

above me
on the wall is a painting which is a still life
of a cauliflower on top of a suitcase with a bunch of keys hanging
from the ceiling above it and I'm curious about the circumstances
which would lead a person to hang their keys from a string
above a suitcase on which they have placed, of all things
a cauliflower and I'm wondering if it's metaphor
or just arrangement

surely no-one would use as obvious a metaphor as a bunch of keys

gurling winds have been predicted
for later today and already the trees
are thrashing in the street outside and there's a gowling
in the chimney of the library's no-longer-used fireplace
which could be a metaphor but it's not (meant to be)
it's just something that's happening

someone who works in the library has
come through the door of this room and placed
a bowl of sweets at the end
of the long desk at which I'm writing
I wouldn't mind one but I'm not sure of her intention
for the sweets so I don't feel I can just help myself

in the café I often go to they give you a sweet
in your saucer when all you've ordered is a cup of coffee
I usually sit inside the café and watch
the same pigeon stotting about under the outside tables
its beak tapping the pavement for crumbs
you can tell it's the same pigeon
because it's so touslie and mauchless

and there's something sad about its being
alone under the tables looking for crumbs among the melancholy legs
of men who also go to that café and sit clacking and smoking outside
while I sit inside (looking through the window at the pigeon
and their legs)

of course
for all I know the pigeon
might be fine and cantie
must at least have a blink or two
of gladness in the dark
under the table, elation
at a cake-crumb or the like

and indeed the men (whose legs
I have described as melancholy
(even though I'm aware of the pathetic
fallacy) simply because they're enclosed
in synthetic-looking breeks
which have not been too short
when the men were upright and yet
have somehow ridden up when they sat down
way up above their pulled-up ankle socks
almost to their knees)
are probably also content

their clack, for example, is animated
and cheerisome and surely this
communication and not the synthetic trousers
or the pale, maisled legs
is what should be noticed

I've become dootsome
about the way I'm writing this poem

it's starting to sound contrived
(a load of havers
people would say in my country)
when the aim was to be totally *un*-contrived
to write about nothing
other than what was happening
while I was cooried in the library
writing and thinking
but somehow things I'm not thinking
or things I don't think I'm thinking
keep being implied

and maybe to you, reader
there are other things being implied
the way you envisage the library, for example
or what you think the pigeon is meant to symbolise
(nothing, btw)
your brain making and unmaking
different connections, the way
you/I/we constantly compare
one thing to another
in order to define it

bizarrely, a man
has just sat down
at the other end of this desk

his sitting down is not in itself bizarre
but he's brought a bowl of broth with him
and he's eating it (loudly)
a bowl of broth! in the library!

maybe you can see the kinch here
it keeps looking like I've chosen this stuff intentionally
or even made it up (the soup, for example, seems unlikely
and could be seen to relate in some way to the sweets in the bowl
or the painted cauliflower, perhaps even
the pigeon's cake crumbs, or indeed the primordial
broth from which we're all derived)
but really I just mention it
because it's happening

which must mean that *everything* has other meaning
not intrinsic to the thing itself but made by the brain
millions of different meanings
depending on the brain doing the making
and the place/time in which the brain exists
which I suppose is obvious
words and their signifiers and all that
the stuff Chomsky bangs on about in *Transformational Grammar*
a book I haven't read and which I should probably be reading now
or at least ordering from the library
instead of sitting here writing down
things which are
happening as if
there's nothing
better to do

the man is done with his soup and has taken a handful of sweets
from the bowl and put them in his pootch and now he's leaving

I too am about to leave and it's possible that
following the man's lead
I'll also take a sweet from the bowl
on my way out

I'm not going anywhere
interesting, only back home
where I'll probably end up
standing on my doorstep
just like I did yesterday
and the day before
patting all my pootches
and then cowping out my bag
on the pathway
searching again for the keys
which I know I have
but which never
seem to be
where I think
I've put them.

Colour Différance

australian yellow

ancient yellow

fierce yellow

sulphur yellow

summer yellow

safety yellow

fastfood yellow

trombone yellow

rock yellow

yellow-footed

yellow brick road

ochre

british yellow

brittle yellow

royal yellow

chromatic yellow

winter yellow

distant yellow

wedding-veil yellow

bone yellow

saft yellow

yellow-herted

yellow hammer

woad

A Map of Belonging

what do you think of as yours?

your hame has been folded in half torn along the crease
folded and torn   folded   and torn
the   scraps   scattered   armchair hairbrush
wind wise   floorboards board game
                                                     necklace cupboard
                                                     photograph

you find yourself landless   suspended   over ocean
that holds the sky   in its blue   in its grey
while you are held   in the body   of a plane
your own body built around   a dark red heart
that does not   belong   anywhere   anymore

        toothbrush fruit bowl
        teacup dinner plate
        shoe tree dressing table
        photograph

where do your belongings come from?

Below you the floor of the ocean
is transcribed with old sea routes
The holds of boats have always been
stowed with bodies

        you no longer ken   who you are
        keep waiting   for understanding
        for words   to make sense
        you have no photographs
        only memories   of them

Inside the hold   light switch towel rail
another and another hold   schoolbooks coat hooks
Matryoshka black   jewellery box tablecloth
boxes of history   photograph
               windowpane
               photograph

keeking into the boxes   it's sometimes possible
to see the future   to see how this will become
an ancient language   how one day we will   understand
the subterfuge of words   the mistake of the possessive
pronoun   the mistake   of *you*   and *I*

door way photo graph

which box did you come out of?
into which world were you welcomed?
were you welcomed?

Inside the world
another and another world
endless openings
into now

key

photo

all of this is too big for you

the map will not stop

un-

folding

Time Zones for Caroline Madden

We chitchat like a pair of scissors, years
of separation no match for growing up
together. Empty glasses shuffle
into the crowd on the table.

Outside it's raining ice. Electric
snowflakes strung across dark.
The pub window lays its white
blanket on the pavement.

We cut and cut until it's yesterday
and I love how my tongue thickens
my mouth rounding out vowels
like it used to. This wholeness.

Across the world it's tomorrow and
my new home is burning. Fire eats
all the animals. We are
too late to stop it.

But for hours now it's long ago
when home was a safe place
– no sleekit landlord
fumbling his lump of coal.

Ice rain falls. The scissors
sneck back and back. Look at the new
dress we made! It could be a bonny dress.
It could be a cloak of flames.

leaves – houses – faces – this day
like all the others and not
at all the scrapsoftime like sheep
-ticks hanging on, getting fatter

No Alarms and No Surprises

Nothing happened really or else
everything kept on happening

I ordered a decaf latte and
a vegan focaccia
leaves did their little manoeuvres
a police car sang through traffic
people wheeled briefs to the courthouse
I broke my glasses (accident)
I broke my bread (deliberate)
clouds squeeried the sky I wrote this poem
someone used the atm someone with noise
-cancelling headphones waited at the crossing
Radiohead played from the café speakers

I'm stowing it all in a bag
handing it over to you

You've got to make it up
because nobody knows what's going on e.g.
all-the-time underground trillions
of chemolithitrophs are thriving without light
eating only stone more of them than
all of life on the surface

what's that got to do with anything?
nothing just me
skrauching across the abyss

Dear John,   a reply to John Forbes's 'The Venice Letters'

Stand roughly here you said and   I am

              and it's   me

                        who's full

                        of holes

                        I know

everyone is

the same

as places are

technicolour or monochrome

        depending on

        perception so   I think

                  I am

                    standing here

                    roughly

or here   some place

        which is mostly TV

                static

                while   I am

                    mostly holes

                    the rest is all

                    white spaces

            I   can't seem

                    to colour in

           so I   photograph

                    and photograph

                    till all my borders blur

Yours,

DNA

rain typewriting
the street and
my body with its history
making me
wet   *(shut up in the audience!)*
the sleekit wink of human DNA
60% the same as banana

Chaplin says to make
the old banana peel joke
funny, show the person
approaching then the peel
then the person spanging
over the peel and disappearing
down a manhole
                         it's raining
in this poem so the pavement
is slippy but that's not important
because I'm not there anymore
I am down
at the crust
of the sea
in the dark
with my ain folk

that's history
for you
          (canned laughter)

QWERTY

ocht, ahm only askin
tae be seen
ahm fed up
bidin in this hoose
wi its durty windaes
the cracks
atween floorboards
fully crums
an shaddies

ahm writin fast
a poyum aboot
a kwik broon fox
but the day is hevvy-lidded
ah need tae gang soon
could ye no fast
-forrard tae the good bits?

hey, whae's there
anyhoo?
(askin furra freend)

There Is a Bigger Telling That Moves Around The World

In Britain, rain like newsprint   the poor getting poorer   something
that might have been done   was not done   and the cold NO of it echoes

on site, builders   in plastic hats   digging, drilling, lifting, building
muscles flexing   and relaxing   in Paleolithic rhythm

and shouting!   they must shout   above the rain's stramash
above pneumatic pounding   and the rackle of spades   opening the ground

here in South Australia, sun centre-spreads   across the sky's page   a backdrop
to our backyard bbq   radio buzzing with stories of asylum seekers   denied their asylum

the dwaiblie muscles of our tongues   flake words like flint   into the afternoon
words that sinter   into the tumulus of kenning   that will be mounded over us

we ken that all we have   is because of mistakes   cellular mishaps   accidents
of birth   all the taking and taking   history's cruelties   right here in the dirt

but over by the bbq   someone is helping a child   flip the meat   passing a spatula
saying *spatula*   and when the child says *badala*   replying *that's right, spatula*

there is a song of YES   in our blood   the ultimate thump-thump of it
the unkindnesses that happen   are not the hindmaist thing   that will happen

we have all the words   and we'll use them   just see how we will.

The Real Me

I wanted to write a poem that didn't end, and to bide inside it. I
would keek out its windows and see sunlight the colour
of bells. (It wouldn't be raining because what is real
is too often hidden by rain.) I would wave to anyone
who happened to stroll past. 'This is who I am!' I would shout
to them and their warm smiles of recognition would make me feel
lived in. I would call my parents from the old bakelite phone, its wires
                                        unspooling the miles between us.
And although there would be nothing but crackle squeezing in
through the holes of the receiver, I would get the feeling
they were listening as I cradled the mouthpiece, mouthing into it
all those things I had always meant to say, trying to iron out
the trousers of truth and memory. I would hum old folk songs
as I prepared nutritious meals, marvelling at the variety
of utensils left behind by previous tenants:

                                   a wooden spurtle, cracked
because it was being used to wedge open the sliding sash window
an early '50s mixer, beaters still caked with antique mix.
When it got dark I would make my way to the attic
where the only sounds would be the distant hammer
of a neighbour's late-night DIY and mice
                                    (okay, maybe I mean rats)

nattling at structural timbers. Of course, an iron bedstead
edged with night blue dropped from a skylight. Tartan slippers
would pose side by side under it. I would crawl beneath
the blankets and hold them around my shoulders, my fingernails
gripping the woollen fibres.
The night's grey footsteps would fitter around the room but the
heavy wardrobe door in the corner would remain firmly closed
hiding all the masks and costumes brattled together on their
hangers.

I would feel safe until
I woke and wanted to go outside. That's when I would discover
the front door was a trompe l'oeil door, the windows impossible
to open wider than a mouth. Standing in front of the glass, I would
catch sight of my neighbour's house, its windows painted onto
brick with the 2D image of my neighbour looking out at me
as a skirp
        then a sowp
            then a blatter
                of rain
                    plowtered down between us.

Seen Through   after Robert Creeley

1. living room window

strain to see beyond this square, to see through
density of learnt words, through all the layers
of eye's lens/prescription glasses/rain-spattered glass
of 'my' living room window/another layer of rain behind it
pushing stitches through sky's material/the distant strata
of summer-burnt trees, dark against the wet-black hills
and a closer layer – 'my' reflected image on top of the living
room reflection (TV from Gumtree, cupboard from hard
rubbish) and in the background daughter standing
in the doorway, calls to me so I turn round, still
holding in behind my een the layers and layers

2. B&B window

this window's different, bigger, wider, the layers not vertical
(lens/glass/rain) but horizontal (sand/sea/sky) and technicolour
like '70s postcards, boats in background sailing to shore
though here there's also a television, its window stowed
with politicians, learnt hand gestures and open/shut mouths
till picture changes to one of the soaps (*Neighbours* maybe
or *Home and Away*) and since arriving at the B&B
I haven't been able to find the remote and can't work out
how to shift channels or what to do with the clarty
towels, which soap we brought and which was here
what's ours to give or take away

3. hilux window

travelling through the desert landscape, south to north
on the Oodnadatta stretch, land smack-flat to all horizons
skooshing windscreen of 4x4, switching wipers to clear
the muck of truck in front but just end up with slaiks
of mud and nothing clearer, though we can see the bloated
bodies of roadkill roos, small paws folded in an X
laid on top of soft white bellies, heavy sky of coming storms
(or maybe one already passed), whirling devils
made from dust, sprays of dust our wheels are making
and yes we know there are clicks and more clicks still to go
before we sleep   *for christ's sake, drive*

4. tent window

we're here and yet we're not, heart of the country
but we're in a resort in hired tent with plastic window
facing Uluru but view's obscured by a tourist shop
its window full of souvenir tat: snow globes/sun
hats/postcards/posters/placemats/coasters/
travel mugs/tourist maps/shopping bags/backpacks/
tea towels/t-shirts/keyrings/kids' toys/
calendars/car charms/colouring books/storybooks/
sticker books/bumper stickers/ballpoints/wallets/
sunglasses/nip glasses/pint glasses/plastic models/
stubbie holders/headscarves/wristbands and sanitary wipes

5. pub window

heading back through country towns, we stop and search
for somewhere to eat so not looking out but keeking
in through sand-etched glass of historic pub, at on-off
flicker and flash of the pokies, rise and fall of gamblers'
arms and further in at folk playing pool, stacks of shrapnel
balanced on the edge, Brownian motion of coloured balls
a giant screen of karaoke, 8-ball bouncing over singalong
words until we take a few stramps back and it melts away
inside the reflection of pioneer high street/colonial homes/
old emporiums/town hall pillars that also melt and turn
to nowt as evening sky empties out its light

6. living room window

today warm wind stirs up slow movement
dust of 'our' backyard skirling round with grushy sand
and brown-edged petals, clouds hushling over distant hills
still only half-seen (so much between – though window
is open there's the mesh of flyscreen and white
sheets sclapping like sails in wind and verandah posts
holding solid roof trusses and rusted galvo over me inside)
but daughter outside, takes down washing, stops to look
at far-off landscape, looks beyond
this square, these layers, to all the
open

Wherever This Is It's Where We Are   after Terrance Hayes

The southern tip of a southern land where all that matters is tonight
at the Wheaty, thedarkthatsurroundsus & words. Under a cosmos of
fairy lights, high on Sonic Prayer IPA, we're waiting for what's
to come. L is waving to someone at the bar but no-one is waving back.
H is on a burstit sofa, sinks so far in we have to hoick her out.
Then everyone reads & it's like Tea Tree Gully with its overlapping
tracks, like Bowden's pavements with their patterns of red brick
like Linear Park with its riverrunsthroughit, like we're travelling
each other's paths. B calls us pilgrims of dust. J tweets bits of poems
& people in other cities in other countries read them. T is fond
of the crow's black heart but his lungs are as light & white as angels
& they fly so tinydelicate from his mouth. Our hair is blond & brown
& grey & we ache in different ways & it is so fuckingbeautiful & sad
the way we bear it. Someone says thank god for cut & paste. Hell
we all say it – it's life after all! D plays the soundtrack from *Basquiat*
at the Barbican & we're filled with it and boomforreal, ohyesweare.
We are the idea of Earth & the idea of earth. It's like the inside
of an internal organ, the fleshy mess of LIFE that keeps on happening
& happening even if we close our eyes. We could be painted in oils
sitting along one side of this long table with our beer & wine & food-
truck burritos. Outside there's the ping of trams shuttling Port Rd
their overhead wires fizzing & sparking, & the labyrinth of dark
streets, alleys, passageways, spidering on through the whole city
down to the beach where allthewaterintheworld
keeps breathing, in & out, regardless.

Deguëllo   after Jeffrey Smart, 'The oil drums' (1992), oil on canvas

Behind the barricade of oil drums, the bugle can still be heard, slink and golden, pinching the folds of sky. It begins as a mewling sound, begins as a melting sound, begins with fracture begins with cracking, begins with the sound of lost things keening in the dark.

Inside the towers behind the oil drums, ears are covered against the sounds of dead bees and rubber trees falling, ice melting, moaning whales, the sound of extinction, the sound of exploitation, the last few notes of the great barren reef.

The bugle plumps up in a crescendo as loud as follicles riven from roots as loud as mayhem, as loud as burning, as loud as the sound of no mercy, no mercy as loud as the long fermata of sun pouring itself through holes.

A crescendo which ends diminuendo, which ends as a reckoning, which ends as a wind which ends with ashes torn and scattered, ends with a caught breath, ends with a whimper finally stops with the crushed bones of small opposable thumbs.

the whole damn thing
keeps on birling, same-old-same-
old memories whispering *this is
who you are* – like that's a thing!

Vixen

This here is the beast of me
snooking round my dark
-shaped den, scutching a dust bath
of foxy stench, hungering
for something sacramental
among the scrammled
bones of lust.

Through small holes
I pech the air
I piss the water and pump the blood
I watch the skies as they open and shut
and know this is
the heart
of all there is.

My yearning streeks the length of me
arches the cathedral
of my back. I accept
my own communion as I
straddle the earth, bend
towards the earth, lick
the sacred longing of my hollows.

Wrong Season Easter

Days pass.
Delicate skies.
Brittle sunrays.

The pardalote chick
on the path outside my house
runkles slowly in on itself.

Feathers loosen and lift
inner solids turn liquid, then gas
skin dips – a sling of flesh – a palimpsest.

Now there are only
wishlists of bone
the thin yellow cold

that brattles through them
and the slow persistent tapping
of branches on the window

like the sound of an egg tooth
worrying away at the fragile
protective shell.

Cemetery Songs

here is a doorway   here is a returning

In time

               graves

                              begin

                                              to sink in

leaving hollow   gaps   at the surface   like the spaces
between   the frail notes   of a half-remembered song
for Eurydice.   We peer into them   beginning to doubt
who we are   and knowing   that if   we look
too long   we'll leave ourselves   behind in the dark.

we are the shadow-ghosts   we are the grainy

In the distance, the funeral
        cortege, travelling the white
                paths of Cheltenham cemetery
                        colour-bled and wavering in
                                the Styxian heat haze, like the
                                        old days when the world was
                                sepia and the only sound was
                        crackle and faded grainy faces
                glanced towards and away from
        an unseen observer who has now
        become us, watching, though
                sometimes glancing away from
                        the screen when the corners of
                                our eyes catch the shadow ghosts
                                        watching us from the hinterlands.

here is a pathway   trampled with voices

The air   we breathe
has passed   through the lungs
of the dead &   we trail long threads
of their silver words   round the labyrinth
of our brain. It helps   to mark the pathways.
Brandishing our   sword of language
like a shiny pin   in the haystacked dark
we carry on   the search for Asterion
sometimes   catching the distant roar
of his lonely   dream which draws us
closer to   the beautiful empty
at the   centre.

the way everything is   like

a balance of substance & space (that impossible nothing
holding things together   & apart) like the crumbling
words on gravestones   & the spaces   in between
the same   words & letters   scushled around
on different stones   into different patterns   like
the stories we are   made of   rearranging &
rearranging   inside us   until they come
to settle   in the ground   like ancient pollen
the small silver   of the rain   falling
patiently   through them   the slow
                                        undoing
                        of everything

                the silver

        in everything.

here is an old tale   repeating, repeating

Like Sisyphus we focus on the boulder's uphill roll
our hands chaffing constantly the surface of
the rock, forgetting the star debris crannied
inside it, deaf to the echo of old songs
thrumming among the constellations.
All we catch are a few frail notes, audible
when we reach the peak & the rock slips
from our grip, spins an instant, the silver
inside it singing before skiltering back
down the pockmarked hillside
back to the bedrock
of endings/
beginnings.

there is beautiful   singing somewhere

END HERE the light.

beyond

wings

its silver

is   the   sky   spreading

presence & absence   & all that   we hold below

of mourning   bodies torn and scattered   notions of

beasts with gowping mouths   the black & gold pageantry

cauls of death   broken stones of old grief   three-headed

START HERE Above the grubby   cherubim   swathed in their skybald

Wrong Season Christmas

Almost a fortnight over 40.
Bushfires celebrate
in neighbouring valleys.

Nerve ends prinkle like tinsel
looped along trembling
branches of bone.

The Magi are travelling towards us
their arms full
of dreadful gifts:

the smell of burning gum
glistering embers of gold
the giant fires that birl inside.

All that wrapped stuff
in the corner
turns quietly invisible.

We hunker by a window
our bodies transparent
and lighter than life.

Frames of Inertia

0 0 1

When I woke, the stars were still
ringing. Crystal clear, as if their years
were nothing.

Darkness lay on the ground
like snow, covering
everything.

I could see your footprints in it
mizzling into distant
nothing.

I spent the morning
hunting but your tracks
were gone, buried

under daylight.
Today is weak, like gauze.
I hold my fear

up to the light like this, see
how it catches?
A version of me

alone at the sink, my hands
in grave-coloured
water. Time with its rifle

eye. Can't I forget
everything, be pre-born
suspended in a globe

that isn't burning
or drowning

010

Is it okay to ask where you are?
The train is travelling towards
you, but you're not

there anymore. Landscape
whidders past windows
in different weights of green

growing away from me. My shoes
are black holes, under
the table/above

the rushing tracks. Impossible
to tell if you're truly
at rest or moving

at uniform velocity.
Childhood moves
so fast, all

the lumps and greens of it
overlapping – birthday candles
knitted jumpers, the cool

of your hand, measuring
my fever, mending
my torn clothes.

Is it okay to say
I am lost
?.

0 1 1

Going back to the terminal
last on the plane. The flight
into breathless

suspension in white. Air
holding us up. Air inside
us. The body

a suitcase
for carrying air.
Cabin crew miming

emergencies. Later positioning
into descent. The stomach hop
as I drop lower.

Below, fire raging through bush
sounds like
unwrapping. Now

I know we're no longer
) but-there's-so-much-left
unsaid-

did-I-tell-you-how-beautiful-
it-was-did-I-tell-you-I-miss-
you-oh-and-here-are-all-

the-gifts-I-didn't-send (travelling
at the same speed

.

How It Is

Like an orb weaver holding fast to its vast maths, the shivering lines stretched over great distances, the spider alone at the centre, quivering

No   no wait   not like that

Like rain falling and falling, drop after drop gathering along threads of web like strings of pearls, no, glass beads, no, tears, like tears, the weight of them so heavy the web must snap, but only sags, the tears sliddering drop after drop into earth

No   no wait   not like that

Like gathering firewood in the rain, the soft impact of drops on your back rough twigs slipping daggers into your fingers, the rain like seeds no, smoke, no, shrapnel, burying itself in your clothes

No   no wait   not like that

Like gum leaves as kindling, their quick crackle, unzipped heat opening orange wings
then runkling back into charcoal and smoke, sinking and rising, to earth, to sky
the tragic theatre of fire

No   no wait   not like that

Like turning from the fire and seeing her in the doorway
with the light of the house skiring around her
her shape in the doorway with the light

Like turning towards the doorway and expecting
like turning towards the door and
like turning towards

no-one

No   no wait   not like that
not like that
wait

The System Won't Save Us (an unlucky sonnet)

Not the white of everything nor everything white
not our date and place of birth nor our current address
not triage nor admissions, not emergency nor recovery
not the far-off skrauching baby nor next door's throttled cough
not the steady Morse of monitor nor the jig-jag line of BPM
not the silver glint of wheelchair nor the rubber thrust of wheels
not the cupboard of folded blankets nor the trolley of mawkit sheets
not the repetition of Spirigel nor Spirigel repetition
not the blood coming out nor the transfusion in
not the pale saline drip nor the dark catheter bag
not the blue procedure mask nor the red box of ECG dots
not the clanjamfrie of corridors nor the colour-coded paths
but an exit sign, white on green, a wee figure moving towards a door

Ars Poetica in the Outback

Roadsong
We've been driving this road for days
eyes drowned in the same of it, the long and the straight
extending and extending into what
cannot be seen. We keep on regardless
except for all the forsaken things that are
scattered at either side – crow-plundered
road kill, burnt bloodwoods, distant erratics
adrift on the sand – these make us stop
get out of the car and lift the camera
holding tight to what is seen through the lens
knowing we must let go of the fliskie
things that scuttle away from the borders
of a frame, leave them to roam the land
unfettered by meaning, purpose or name.

Sandsong
Here in the desert, distance and
the flat land curve the horizon so we
ken we're on a planet. The moon's theme tune
plays but there are no giant steps. Here
our footprints are blown into dust. We are self-
weighted, bodies drawn irresistibly
towards the hot interior. What is
it we are doing here? Trying to mend
dust? To bend it into a foisted narrative
as if death could be fixed, as if we could
remake our dark into some kind of sense?
We trinkle it into our hands like
we're weighing it, its worth, to understand
our mauchtless incline towards the earth.

No Matter What

today ahm alive, taes
pointin taewards
ooter space where
we're aw gaan
anyhoo
that's fur anither
time noo is sticky
wi sun
light and fallin
socks long blacks
flat whites the glitter
o birds an bricks
an tram song
an poyums
ready
tae munch on

an mibby
the morn

One Thing and Another   for Jill Jones

The neighbour's magnolia is
a bairn's alphabet. That camel's hump
your stowed-out inbox. Samphire is
the dear blood travelling home. Uluru
a ringing phone. That clicking down of gears is
the Cuillin range. Tim Tams are
carols in the snow. Those sky lights

                        are a cross
                        are an emu's footprint
                        are alien invaders
                        coming to steal our jobs.

The big M for Macca's is a curlew
scrying through haar. The turtle's wake
your first ever word. That thraw in your chest

                        is exactly the same
                        as solid puddles
                        smattered into stars.

You make it what it is.
You make it what
it is.
You make it. You
make it.

Semiosphere   for Rachael Mead and Heather Taylor Johnson

1: Umwelt

I have seen a fox move
in silence through the city
and this I ken

          the trees breathe the fox
          and the wet black pavements
          shine for it

say what you will
about this world or the next
       some things
       are kent
       without kenning

                    the fox kens
             as it moves through the silence
                breathing the trees
                and the pavements

the rain runs in rivers
through its red-black fur
and the pavements are thick
with its foxy scent
and the rain rises
to meet it as it runs
and the pavements run
with rivers of its redness

       other worlds hurtle through
       its black-red eyes

              and then it's gone
              leaving a shadow _____

2: Corporeal

eyes
tapetum lucidum
tapetum lucidum
its eyes are amber planets
and I see through them

                                    I see through
                                to the other side

tail
mind widening – touching the brush
the bristly quivering tips
and the deep-down
soft stuff

                                                feet
                                it panders the old pathways
                                        circling silence
                                feet listening to the nothing
                                    and the everything
                                        it comes from

heart
a dark livid thing
dunting dunting
like the iron hammer
at the Earth's core

——————————————————————————————> smoking and stamping
                                            in the air

3: Liminoid

there wiz a bunch o us there wiz davy whae wiz a lot older an some
kindae accoontant an sharon an stacey the pole dancers an forbes
whae wiz rich an went tae the posh school an aw the rest o us whae
hud left the club an were headit fur the party an we wur doiterin doon
dundas st which is oan a hill in whit's cried the new toon in edinburgh
tho it looked awfy auld tae us wi its georgian hooses an thur ded strait
lines the long row o thum aw the way doon the hill an the dark windaes
starin at us frae either side an us a tousie bunch in the middle o the
street wi the music o the club still duntin in oor blood and the thocht o
the party pumpin in oor veins and the freedom o walkin in the middle
o the road cos it wiz early mornin an there wiznae enny traffic yet an
it wiz wunnae them streets that if it hud been daylight we wouldae
been able tae see the firth o forth glentin in the distance and beyond
the firth fife so that even in the hauf-dark we still kent there wiz that
muckle stretch o water movin perpendicular tae us somewhere far off
an we wur aw laffin aboot sumhin when ah looked up in the direction
o the firth an there wiz a fox crossin the road ahead o us sillooetted
in the skreich o day its tapered neb an delikit legs the thick bush o
its tail an the minnit ah seen it it stopped in the middle o the road an
looked taewards us or as ah thocht then an ah suppose still think noo
taewards me and naebiddy else hud seen the fox so there wiz still aw
the racket goin on aroond me but there wiz a pencil line o silens runnin
atween me an the fox an it felt like we were staunin in a forest like the
ghost o the old forest that lies aneath the city hud sprung up aroond us
as we stood there lookin at each ither an then the fox turnt back tae its
path cairried on its jurney an ah cairried on mine an fur sum reesin ah
said nuthin tae ayebiddy else like did you see that or look a fox or enny
o the things I micht hae expected masel tae say instead ah jist cairried
on but ah hud it inside me that pencil line o silence an still sumtimes
ah kin feel it there when there's noise aw aroond me ah feel its taut
string huggerin the silens an ah think o it as a gift frae the fox

4: Liturgy

sometime us earthy
sometime us blood
bone-white and soil-black
hunger deep want has

        brothers and sisters
        deep in the black ground
        inside me rise they
        soil-black and heart-pound

old is the kenning
deep in the heart-pound
silent the earth-speak
deep in the black ground

        blood in the heart-pound
        blood in the tongue-mouth
        blood in the tooth-drip
        blood in the black ground

ayoo my brothers
ayoo my sisters
wake you and sleep you
in heart-pound, in black ground

5: Parousia-apousia

I stotter through clumsy logic, fox
thoughts thick with sticking-plaster blood clots
scabs ripped and clinging to the cross-hatched fabric
car-crash mesh inside the windscreen of my skull
my eyes are crazed like paving
reticulated retina
      reticular formation
           messed   responding
           to all the wrong
               stimuli

      you solve me fox, you straighten my gaze
      push your bright dark neb through my CNS

you scent-mark me, make sense of me
pack me with my quidditas
  you show me the wind
          and the sound of the wind
        wind that lifts
      the scattered scraps
       birls them about inside itself
          a pre-paradigmatic pottery
           a lottery of hermeneutics
        it's how we are and we are not
      all dotted inside
   the world's Mandelbrot set
     fractals of endless synecdoche
        ravelling, unravelling
          like string

you show me the ice on the leaves, ice that thickens
    and rugs the leaf down, you show me the ice

                        and the weight of the ice
                    that rives the stem from the branch

                                    and drops
                        splinters fracturing silence
                            fractions of silence

            splintering time, you carry this in your eyes
                you put the ice shards into mine
                    we clink our eyes like ice-filled glasses
                        bay our slainte to the crescent moon
                        we croon, we drone, we are fou
                        fox, I love you like a sibling
                            you are there for me
                            I think you are
                                pandering through
                                    my peripheral I

I turn my head and you're gone
but you're always there all the same

drawing my eyes   towards the song
towards the baton   the beating of time
you are there, fox   you are not there, fox
you are not there   you are

6: Consummation

I inside everything
and silence

having learnt a thing's name
having used its name
I'd like to learn its silence
to be thirled with skraiks of silence
to be threaded with webs of silence
to have my bones picked clean of noise
and my blood filled with silence
to see the way it is and ken I cannot say it
and to pack my mouth
with silence

silence of trees and hedges and grass
and pavements' and streetlights' silence
silence of earth and stones and coal
and gold and bones and rain's silence
silence of daybreak, silence of dusk
silence of forests, silence of fur
silence of heartdunts, silence of breath
silence of sand dunes, silence of skulls
silence of singing, silence of claps
cities' and rivers' and oceans' silence
molecules' and mountains' and midnight's silence
the silence of everything
folding   into
leaving   only

silence

so noisy, so beautiful
these scraps of torn fabric
this patchworkliving
these finite days

Vessel for Adrian

I

No-one else has seen inside this bairn.

She's just wee. The sky   does not yet curve down
around her. It is still   contained
in a blue strip   at the top of the page.

She's setting her place   for breakfast
but has stopped   halfway between
the crockery cupboard   and the table.

The sun is just risen   above the roof of her building
so that she can see the reflection   of her windows
in the windows   of the building opposite.

She doesn't ken   it's a reflection.
It seems a thing of itself   a thing that appears
and disappears   with the light.   In her hands

a cup is moulded   around its cup-worth of space.
In her head   something is rugging   at the reins
of the kitchenette   clock.

She has asked her mother   a question.
When you get older   do you remember more?
And her mother has answered   *Aye, I suppose you do.*

The bairn kens   this is the wrong answer.
She kens her mother   means you have more things
to remember, there's more living   filling your head

but what the bairn means   is will she remember
being born   will she remember
where she was   before she was   born?

She doesn't ken how   to ask the question.
Instead, she has stopped   to remember
this   forever:

her hands cooried   around a space
she is carrying to a table   a cup
inside which   reflected light pings.

She watches her hands move   apart.
She watches the cup drop   and break
the pieces spanghewing   in different directions

making new   angles of light   forming
the beginning of kenning   how we go   beyond   what we are
an awareness   of being and not being

a first meme that will repost   versions of itself
in her brain   until she comes to see that
the cup isn't   what matters.

II

It's lunchtime.   They're still in bed.

When the morning was   thinner
they went foraging   running naked
to the kitchen   reenging

through cupboards   for cereal
eating it   straight from the packet.
They raided the fridge   and kissed

with mouths full   of strawberries, yoghurt
the pink-white mess   of their tongues.
Now she has woken into   the middle

of the day.   The sun has tension   spinning
its heat   into a rope that warps through   the window
down onto her belly   an umbilical cord

drookit with roaring.   He's asleep on his stomach
beside her   the dip and rise of his arse   the blond hairs
pushing up through   his skin. In her belly

the roar comes from way back   from out of the mud
-sucking swamps   a roar or grunch that says *hungry*.
She wants to call it love   but it's not that waffie

human thing.   It's grander. Almost geological.
Not of her making   something from the dark ages
lingering   in the background

like cosmic microwaves.   It must have been there
when Paleolithic hominins   were fucking
in forests and caves   all matted hair

and ugsome nails, their outlines   like faded
daguerrotypes imprinted   within her silhouette.
It must have been there when   Chaucer's medieval

couples were fucking   in pigpens and haystacks
the skirmish of petticoats   the clap of leather aprons
their peching breath still here   filling her lungs.

He wakes and rises   on the opposite side   of the bed
uncurtaining the windows   he lives behind.
She sees herself wee inside them   and he draws her

further in until   their skin is sliding like rain
the tectonic grind   of their pelvic collision
hands   cupped around each other.

Her head is so full   questions inside questions
things she doesn't know   how to ask. But she knows
there is nothing   bigger than this:

hunger and fulfilment   fucking
and sleeping and waking   the filling
and emptying   of the world.

III

They're together   at the table.

The skin-and-bones of their meal   is in front
of them. Striations   of tomato sauce stripe
their plates, showing the pathways   of their chips.

His reading glasses sit   cross-legged
on the scrubbed wood. In the lenses   the refraction
of his face is much smaller   than his actual face

the same way that she holds   only the totiest
image of him in her mind   never kenning
who he is, who she is   where they stop and

where the outside begins.   She touches the back
of his hand where the star   at the centre
of their universe   has touched it

runkling and freckling   leaving its mark.
He knots his fingers   around hers.
Behind him   the kitchen door is open.

An earlier rain has pixelated   the flyscreen
making a pattern   like a calendar
with some of the days   exed in.

From outside comes the racket   of crickets
sawing through   the evening's minutes
splitting them into   their infinite parts.

She lets go his fingers   and watches
her hands move in   around her cup
which is full   of tea. She blows down on it

so that the surface   coruscates into miniature
waves that break   against the inside edges
and switter back   to the centre.

She thinks of the soundwaves of crickets
moving   the hammer and anvil in her ear
to send   their song to her brain.

Wind blows through the flyscreen   popping empty
some squares of water   changing the cross-stitch.
She feels the skirr   of outside

pigeons' feet prattling   on the tin roof
blowflies ellipsing the porch light
like planets.   Even the spaces   between

blades of grass in the lawn   are alive:
beetles, grubs   stoor, stones
seeds, roots   all the totie things

doing their work.   Sky in her een
cup in her hands   she wonders
what is   hers?

Connections

The diagnosis is hard
to hear. Dark
flames lap the future's pretty
cottage. Knees and elbows
smoulder anger. Three streets
away a fire engine's
high-pitched gape
sounds among the traffic.

The grasshopper in the bathroom. I trod on it in socks, not smushing it but breaking off a leg and not noticing until I sat on the milky bath edge in half-light and a small movement came to me. I peered closer – *what is that?* – and saw the wee thing crawling around its broken leg, nudging it with its head as if trying to coax it into life circling and circling, touching it. I felt what I thought must be its confusion and grief and my throat was thick with what I'd done. Its poor big eyes. I didn't know how to make amends.

On the other side
of the apartment wall
our neighbour is crying.
No-one can hear her.
Not true, we can hear her
but we don't ken her so we don't
ken how to help her.
We wonder why
nobody helps her.

My boy when he was a bairn. A few days after I'd told him that wild things want to stay in the wild, he came skelping in from the garden his breath crosshatched with sobs, and threw his arms about me pressing his head into my belly. *Whatever is it?* I asked, my fingers stroking the dachshund bones of his spine. *I let all my caterpillars go* he said. *I put them back in the wild.*

Birds also have emergencies.
Their loud alarms in backyards
and bushland. And that half-dead
galah, flattened on tarmac, attended
by ten or so others who breeshled
into the road to flutter and skraik
around it whenever there was
a break in the traffic.

The butterfly in my parents' bedroom. When I was a bairn I would run to their room on Sunday mornings and coorie into the soft place where warmth pooled. One morning, a butterfly flew in through the open window and I leapt up laughing, clutching at the colours until my fingers closed around it and it dropped on their covers. I picked up the broken thing, sobbing, smoothing the runkled wings and hoping they might mend. I can still hear the low murmle of my parents' comfort, feel their hands on my hottering back, a memory from the actual event, or the way I pictured it whenever the story was told, or maybe just the way I'm picturing it now, as I write this stopping sometimes to chaff at my burning joints while my parents lie asleep in a bed so far away I can no longer run to it, can no longer find its soft place.

Arrival for Katherine Tamiko Arguile

When we finally reach
the mangroves, the thrang
of trees sinders out into unobstructed water
                              the trees
                          untangling   into
                                              air

threads hanging from branches
like cut   puppet strings
the canopy of leaves like the dropped

                              shroud
                    of a no-longer-needed
                      deus ex machina.

We hardly ken what to do
with all the light that keeps happening
the open palm of the water uplifted, heezing the light
                          up among the trees
                    trunks deepening into
                          the water, into
                the sand, the long threaded roots
                              assembled in jazzy
                          patterns.   .

Here, everything trembles:
        rainbow lorikeets in the leaves above us
            orb weavers on invisible webs
                swallowtails in the blossom.

            The only thing that is solid and still is
                the clagginess of a white cocoon
                    stuck to the bark in front of us.

We look back
through the fankle
of trees and there's no sign
of the path we took, just the weight
of all the time we wasted   shifting

                                    inside us
                            gathering in our eyes
                                and dropping into
                        the water at our feet
                                saying

                        I'm sorry

                I'm sorry
I didn't use this properly
I did nothing
big with it.

The water leams it
                            back into our eyes as if to say
                                    hey! everything's
                                        made of little
                                            – the littleness
                                    is what makes it
                                bonny
and we see how the thrang of trees
comes down to the one
whose roots
we find purchase on
                        and the reflection
                                of that tree in the water
                                    and the reflection
                                    of the reflection
                        in our eyes

and how the thrang of creatures
zooms in to one totie specimen
asleep in a cocoon
sweeled in the furlongs
                          of
                               thread
                                    it has spun
                                         around
                                                 itself

                               waiting
                          inside
                   until
it is ready

                   and we ken
                          that whatever
                               track we took
                                    it didn't
                                         matter
                                         it was always
                                         going to end
                                              with us
                                         standing
                                         in the
                               mangroves

                               our eyes
                   thirled
          with reflected
light.

we're connected, right?
leaves – houses – faces – this day
the whole damn thing
so noisy, so beautiful

ACKNOWLEDGEMENTS

These poems were written on Kaurna land. My deep respect to elders past, present and future. Australia always was and always will be Aboriginal land.

For support in the early years, I'd like to thank Sean Bradley, Todd McEwen, Duncan McLean and Kevin Williamson.

For publishing/reading opportunities and career support in Australia, I would like to thank Ken Bolton, Jelena Dinic, Peter Goldsworthy, Heather Taylor Johnson, Jill Jones, Dominic Symes, Annette Willis and the editors of *Australian Poetry Journal Members Anthology*, *Etchings*, *foam:e*, *Grieve Poetry Anthology*, *Gutter Magazine*, *Irises*, *New Boots and Pantisocracies*, *New Writing Scotland*, *Newcastle Poetry Prize Anthology*, *Plumwood Mountain*, *Rabbit Poetry*, *Raining Poetry in Adelaide*, *Social Alternatives*, *Southerly*, *StylusLit*, *The Disappearing*, *The Evergreen*, *The Poets' Republic*, *Tincture*, *Verity La* and *Westerly*, where some of these poems have appeared.

For friendship and fun through Little Windows, Clarice Beckett and beyond, my thanks to Jill Jones. Also to Kent MacCarter for meticulous, insightful editing of this manuscript.

For great poetry feedback and friendships, the poetry groups EWS (Rachael Mead and Heather Taylor Johnson who introduced me to the wonderful Adelaide poetry scene and helped coax my poetry into shape with laughter, love and fine wine) and Poetica (J V Birch, Mike Hopkins, Cary Hamlyn, Jules Leigh Koch, Jennifer Liston, Louise Nicholas, Krishan Persaud, Russ Talbot, Rob Walker and Liu Wanling) – no better way to spend a Sunday afternoon.

I'd also like to thank my dear friend, senpai and writing companion, Katherine Tamiko Arguile. So glad you're here, lovely hen.

Alison Flett is originally from Scotland. There, she published three poetry collections, one of which was shortlisted for the Saltire First Book of the Year Award. Since her move to Australia, her work has been published in many anthologies and journals including *Cordite Poetry Review*, *Island*, *Southerly* and *Westerly*. She has been longlisted for the ABR Elizabeth Jolley Short Story Prize and the Bridport Short Story Prize, shortlisted for the Whitmore Press Manuscript Award, the Adelaide Festival Unpublished Manuscript Award, The University of Canberra Vice-Chancellor's International Poetry Prize and the Newcastle Poetry Prize. In 2020, she won the Olga Masters Short Story Awards. She is an arts reviewer for *InReview*, commissioning editor for *Transnational Literature* and publisher at Little Windows Press.